Uniquely Me!

A Celebration of Special Needs

Michelle Vanessa O'Reilly

Illustrations by Malina Rose Mixon

WestBow Press books may be ordered through booksellers or by contacting:

WestBow Press
A Division of Thomas Nelson & Zondervan
1663 Liberty Drive
Bloomington, IN 47403
www.westbowpress.com
844-714-3454

Illustrations by Malina Rose Mixon

Scripture quotations taken from The Holy Bible, New International Version® NIV® Copyright © 1973 1978 1984 2011 by Biblica, Inc. TM. Used by permission. All rights reserved worldwide.

ISBN: 978-1-6642-5452-7 (sc)
ISBN: 978-1-6642-5453-4 (e)

Library of Congress Control Number: 2022901832

Print information available on the last page.

WestBow Press rev. date: 2/28/2022

Uniquely Me!

A Celebration of Special Needs

Michelle Vanessa O'Reilly

Illustrations by Malina Rose Mixon

WestBow Press books may be ordered through booksellers or by contacting:

WestBow Press
A Division of Thomas Nelson & Zondervan
1663 Liberty Drive
Bloomington, IN 47403
www.westbowpress.com
844-714-3454

Illustrations by Malina Rose Mixon

Scripture quotations taken from The Holy Bible, New International Version® NIV® Copyright © 1973 1978 1984 2011 by Biblica, Inc. TM. Used by permission. All rights reserved worldwide.

ISBN: 978-1-6642-5452-7 (sc)
ISBN: 978-1-6642-5453-4 (e)

Library of Congress Control Number: 2022901832

Print information available on the last page.

WestBow Press rev. date: 2/28/2022

You see, when I was born, I seemed like a typical baby. I cooed, smiled, and laughed. But, as I grew older, I could not do some of the same things other kids my age could do. My family started to realize that I was not typical or ordinary. Besides learning to crawl and walk long after other babies my age, I had autism. People with autism may look just like everyone else, but they sometimes think, talk, and act differently. Our behaviors can range a lot. For example, when I tried to open my mouth to talk, no words came out!

While sleeping at night, my clothes and bed were always wet in the morning, even as a teenager!

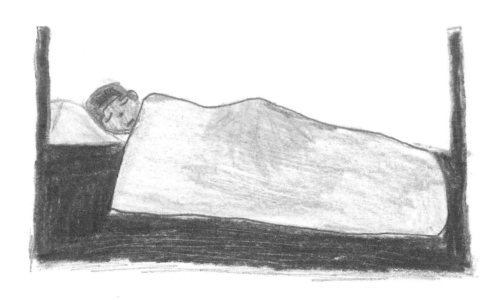

Everyone agreed. *That* was unique.

"He eats like Cookie Monster!" my mother would say as I shoved food into my mouth.

Was being unique becoming a *problem*?

As I got older, I sometimes got frustrated with not communicating correctly. I would occasionally hit or get upset when people did not understand me. I would scream or show how I felt through my behavior. Sometimes, I would get upset in restaurants when I was hungry. I could not communicate that the food was taking too long to come to my table. People would stare as I spilled juice on the table.

"What's wrong with him?" they seemed to
say as they stared and pointed.

Finally, when I was seventeen, I was invited to live in a
group home for boys to get some help. I lived with five
other teenage boys who were also autistic. A group home
is a regular house in a neighborhood, except it has staff
to help us. First, I met a friend who also flapped his
hands when extremely excited. That is called stimming.

Then I met another boy who could not talk. We finally learned
to use a fork correctly even though we were teenagers.
At home, we enjoyed a gigantic swing set and trampoline
in the backyard that was strong as steel for us big boys.
Even the equipment was unique and specially made!

I soon realized it: Everyone in this house was unique!

Together, we learned patience as we learned to pour a drink without spilling it. Next, we learned self-control to stay dry by pointing to a picture on an iPad when we needed to use the bathroom. Lastly, we learned etiquette as we learned to use a fork correctly and eat neatly. I started to give a "thumbs up" and grin as I accomplished tasks and gained independence. Using the iPad to speak was indeed unique and special.

My mom could not see me for a long time because of a deadly pandemic, and no visitors were allowed at my house. When she finally saw me, she was surprised that I could do so many new things. We both giggled and squealed with excitement at the grand reunion! Eventually, I could go to restaurants without making a big mess under and on the table. I could go home for visits, and I remembered to use the bathroom when I needed to.

"He is uniquely special," my mother said.

Like many children around the country, my friends and I had to attend school online. We were so happy to finally break out of our bubble group home and attend school in person! My mother was glad to hug me in the morning as I anxiously boarded the big, yellow bus. I was so happy to be reunited with my teacher and school friends!

Unfortunately, one day Mom received a call that I could not go to school. One of the friends in the home had come down with the coronavirus. Everyone would quarantine. I was back to having no visitors and staying home.

My mom was sad but visited me from the window in the living room as much as she could. The staff pulled down my mask so she could see my face. I was still smiling my super sunny smile! Even though I was nonverbal, my smile hugged her. It said, "Mommy, I'm okay. Don't worry!" Eventually, I was able to go back to school. Sometimes, love doesn't need words. Big smiles, laughs, hugs, and kisses are enough.

Just as God protected Daniel in the lion's den; He sent his angels again to watch us in the group home.

Melina

"For I know the plans I have for you," declares the Lord, "plans to prosper you and not to harm you, plans to give you hope and a future." Jeremiah 29:11. NIV

Always treat autistic people like everyone else. God has a unique plan for each of our lives, even if it is different from our friends. People with autism may not be able to speak or answer to their name, but they can still hear your words and feel your kind heart.

Always trust God. He knows what is best.
You, too, are unique and special!

Glossary

Autism refers to a broad range of conditions. People with autism may have challenges with social skills, repetitive behaviors, speech, and nonverbal communication. It also affects how they relate to the world around them.

According to the Centers for Disease Control and Prevention, autism affects 1 in 44 children in the United States today.

Spectrum: A spectrum refers to a wide range of behaviors. The effects of autism are different for each person.

Stimming: Repetitive motions used to help cope with emotions

Group homes: Group homes are places that provide support for people with disabilities.